Unleashed Rage

Poems and Photography by

Dawn Teresa McKinney

To order additional copies of this book, contact:
Xlibris
844-714-8691
www.Xlibris.com
Orders@Xlibris.com

ISBN: Softcover   978-1-4568-4537-7
        EBook   979-8-3694-3707-0

Print information available on the last page

Rev. date: 12/17/2024

Dedication

To my wonderful mother Teresa Dawn McKinney for your patience during my ups and downs. Thank you for all your support and love. No one will truly know how I am so blessed to have such a tremendous mother like you. I love you so much.

IN MEMORY OF

Uncle Dana Alan McKinney, you are my guardian angel from up

above and you live forever in my heart.

Table of Contents

Broken-Hearted

If I…

If I only knew, that morning kiss good-bye would be our last,
I would have kissed you a hundred times more.
If I only knew, that would have been our last hug,
I would have held you closer.
If I only knew, that would have been the last words I would say to you,
I would have told you, that I love you with all of my heart.

If I only knew, that would have been the last time I could hold your hand,
I would have never let go.
If I only knew, I would touch your face no longer,
I would have done so as gentle as a feather.
If I only knew, that I would call out your name no more,
I would have shouted it out loud for the whole world to hear.

If I only knew, that would have been the last time I would have wiped away your crocodile tears,
I would have saved every last one.

If I only knew, that I would never see you laugh again,
I would have made you laugh forever.
If I only knew, that I would never see you again,
I would have been more grateful for every minute I had with you,

If I only knew, I could not be with you forever,
I would have never let you leave.

If I…
If I only knew!

-2002-

Inside

I smile, laugh, and joke
On the outside
I sigh, cry, and choke up
On the inside

I pretend like everything is fine
But I just want to runaway and hide.
Hide from all the bad people and memories.
And scream at the top of my lungs.

What did I do to deserve these?
Why can't I just close my eyes, and forget everything?
Why can't I just start with a new slate?

I put up a high shield and make it bulletproof
So I can heal,
Heal before I get hit again by another painful memory of my past.

And still I smile, laugh, and joke
On the outside
I let no one see me sigh, cry, and choke up
On the inside

-2002-

Letting Go

Every thought of you that goes through my head,
Leaves me breathless
Knowing you were always near kept me up on that ledge.
Knowing you were gone made me slip and fall.
Finding out you never left, made me start climbing up.
Finding out you have left for good, has my heart breaking
and my soul empty.
Finding someone to love like I loved you is impossible.

Thinking, if only I had sent you the numberless letters I
wrote to you would have changed anything makes me pace.

Not being able to touch your face,
Kiss your lips,
Watch your sips,
Hold you close,
Or hear you boost.

I always had a candlelight burning for you.
And to blow it out now seems like an end.
An end that I'm not ready to face,

No one understands how much I will miss you,

My first true love
My muse
My friend

-2005-

STILLNESS
The public boat dock area on
Lake Placid in
Lake Placid, FL..

The Walk Alone

I walk along a beaten path,
Over and Over
Is it that I am a creature of habit or just scared to
go a new way?

When I come to that fork in the road,
I weigh my options heavily,
Is it that I do what I'm taught or just afraid of
failure?

I push myself far away,
From all the men I have ever known.
Is it that I am cold-hearted or is it just my fear of
rejection?

I've pushed myself away from the one, who
loved me with all of his heart,
To give my heart to the one I thought I loved.
He pushed me as far away from him as I could
go,
Is it that I am doomed to stay alone for all
eternity or am I just faced with reality?

I walk along a beaten path because I am a
creature of habit and have a fear of rejection,

Will I walk alone forever?
Only time will tell me that.

-2003-

Untitled 2000

I know I shouldn't be here.
Wishing,
Hoping,
Waiting

I must be so dumb!
He is never going to come.

Holding my breath,
Will do me no luck,
Unless it leads to death

Ah! Death for me,

To make them see!
To make them see!

It's not a size three that matters,
Only the lonely heart that shatters!

-2000-

Desired

A Dream

Feeling the sun beaming on my face,
Walking through the sand with such grace,
Listening to the seductive sounds from the guitars in the music,
Dancing so close that it looks like we are making love,

In my dreams of Costa Rica with you

Surfing the perfect wave,
Sailing and drinking the days away,
Massaging your body just right,
Kissing you under the moonlight,

In my dreams of Costa Rica with you

Gazing into your deep brown eyes,
Escaping away from all the reality in my mind,
Flickering of the candlelight on the walls shows us,
Making love, passionate love all night through 'til morning's first sight
Waking up each morning from this incredible dream, makes me want to sleep forever
So you and I could forever be in

Costa Rica

-2004-

HELLO NEW DAY
Off Lake Jackson in
Sebring, FL.

A Wonderful Night

As the colorful reddish-orange sunset appears,
The soft sound of jazz music fills the atmosphere.
Myself and the one I love,
Will let our hearts combine to become as one.
While we gaze into each other's eyes,
And tell our deepest fantasies.
Passionately, he pulls me close and
Kisses me a hundred times more,
He caresses my breasts as I softly kiss his lips.
Our bodies entwine like a dolphin's twist.
Candles lit around the bedroom
Showing us the shadows of,

Love making on this wonderful night

Love making causes an enormous heat between us that make,
Little beads of sweat that run down his chest and on to my stomach
Falling asleep in his warm arms,
For the first time, I knew I was with whom I belonged.
Waking up to a vase full of white, long stem, no thorn roses,
A symbol of the purity that our love possesses
That morning sunrise showed ever so brightly with bluish, peach, pink-purple sky,
Made my heart soar way up on cloud nine
As that special night of love making will stay with me always,
Makes me not sad that he had to go away,
For he is still in my heart and will live forever and again

-2002-

ANGEL STAR
Off County Road 635 in
Sebring, FL.

Deep Soul

Some friendships are like sunrises,
They brighten up your darkest days,
Then fade away too soon.

But I feel that our connection is more than a friendship.
It is a connection that is powered by your mystic mind.
Your soul is deep which leaves me thinking for weeks.

Your eyes tell a different story than what you lead on.
Your spirit stands tall and your heart soars high for a selected few.
I thought a person such as you could never come into my life and deeply change me.

For a while, I thought maybe we had twin souls, but as I look closer,
It is just a connection, anything more would be wrong.
Always stick to your morals, when you lose them, you lose your soul.

-2004-

ORANGE PASSION
Off State Road 66 in
Sebring, FL.

Deepest Desire

You are the fire
And I am the wood.
Do everything of my desire,
Hmmm that feels good.

You are the fire
And I am the wood.
Just a bit higher,
Ooh I knew you could.

I am the fire
And you are now the wood.
Let me fulfill your desire
Like you have fulfilled mine

-1994-

RUSHING WATERS
Cypress Gardens Adventure
Park in Winter Haven, FL.

My Connection to You

As the passionate words roll off my tongue,
I write this poem to you with love.

As the longing for you gets ever so breathless,
This deep burning inside me is growing so restless.
As the sun goes down, the sensual passions start to peak,
The hunger grows stronger and I become weak.
It flows inside of me like the eruption of a volcano,
And with every touch from you I begin to quiver.
I can feel every sensation and taste the sweet juices you bring.

I am alive again and I am connected to you!

As our bodies entwine,
I drink your red wine.
I intake all that you possess
And give back twice as much.
I can feel you when you are not here.

I am alive again and I am connected to you!

You can see my soul so clear,
And I can be yours to keep.
You have brought out a side of me,
That has been hidden inside so deep.
My dear, when we see each other once again,
We will embrace and cause a cosmic explosion.
I am alive again and in large part to you!

I am alive and I am connected to you!

-2002-

Which is it?

What is it about my body that you like?
Is it my smooth luscious lips that softly kiss you on your cheek?
Or is it my brown eyes that you look deep inside to see my soul?

What is it about my body that you like?
Is it my nose that smells your scent all over my clothes?
Or is it my ears that hear the sweet nothings that you speak?

What is it about my body that turns you on?
Is it my soft neck that quivers when you kiss it?
Or is it the curves of my bra that covers my breasts?

What is it about my body that turns you on?
Is it my breasts that your hands glide over and slightly grab?
Or is it the nipples that get excited with each gentle lick?

What is it about my body that you like?
Is it the swaying of my hips to the music?
Or is it my shiny golden brown back that you massage so good?

What is it about my body that you like?
Is it my legs that do the strut?
Or is it the roundness of my butt?

What is it about my body that turns you on?
Is it my hands that slowly creep up your legs that makes you rise up for the occasion?
Or is it the moans that I make out of pleasure?

What is it about my body?
What turns you on?
Let us explore these.
Let's explore them now!

-2003-

Unleashed

Aggression

All I see, all I hear, it's all around
All you say, all you do, what's wrong with you?
Hurtful actions, disgusting words, why the lies
Can't you see? Can't you see? This is the real world.

You claim to hide behind the Bible,
You make it seem that you're not liable.
All you do is twist the words,
All you say is you're doing his work.

You hide yourself behind a white robe,
You stand tall and yell out, "Get over here, Boy!"
I can't stand here and let you people run all over me
I have a place on this earth, so you just have to deal.

How can someone, who kills another for the color of his or her skin,
Think that it's not a sin!
You tell me I'm inferior,
And claim you are superior.

You say that anyone who isn't white is less than human
That's not right.
You go around and cold-bloodedly kill
Yet still you think we are the animals.

I'm sick of all the hate!
I'm sick of all the lies!
I wish you people would just realize
That everyone is meant to be different.
You people want to eliminate us
But do, at your own risk
'Cause by the time it's all over
You'll be the one's suffering in HELL at the end!

-2001-

Blinded

You said, you loved me
But you lied.
You said, you would never hit me
So why did I have to hide?
You told me I was imagining it
You told me I was beautiful.
You said, you were the only one for me
You said I could never leave you.

I believed you,
When you said these things,
I was blinded by you,
But now I see the truth.
When you talk to me, I don't hear you.
When you touch me, I don't feel you.
When you stand in front of me, I don't see you.

I am stronger
Now that you are gone
You bother me no longer
You and I are done!

I can't believe I trusted you.
I can't believe I fell for you.
You blinded me,
But now, I finally see the truth.

-2002-

STICKS TO BREAK BONES
Off the back roads of Lake
Placid, FL.

Broken Friendship

As your friend's blood drips on the ground,
Never will we see you frown.
Beat and kick and stab her good,
To show everyone, she doesn't belong in this neighborhood.

All the while, shouting awful racial slurs,
It is beginning to feel like a big blur.
For ten years, you have partied and laughed together,
Shared sorrow and lent each other a shoulder to cry on
But still you stand there with no emotion.

You let everyone around you run your life,
But they will never truly know why you sit up and cry at night.
You have lost the only true thing you ever had,
To a cruel word that can never be taken back.

Like our now broken friendship.

-2002-

Changes

Change is inevitable according to most people,
You change your underwear everyday so you don't stay dirty.
You change the station on the radio because you hate commercials or you want to hear something different.
You may not like something on your body, so you get; lifted, tightened, reduced, added, tucked, or sucked away
Your emotions, habits, life events, the seasons, environment, and the weather all can change at the drop of a dime.

Change *I think to myself, there has to be another solution out there.*

Change can be good and it can be bad or downright just plain uneasy, but it is necessary.
Great leaders like Abraham Lincoln and Martin Luther King Jr. had dreams, strived for them; endured pain and suffering, and eventually their lives were taken for their beliefs for change and freedom.

Change *I say, we are in need for something better.*

All of their blood, sweat, and tears; bruises, scars and fears; but most importantly their dreams have traveled into many minds that helped make powerful transformations into the realities of today.

After eight years of the same old broken promises, let downs, and lies; has risen change.
The people finally took responsibility for themselves and this Great Nation.
Our nation begged for a Change and we will get it this week.

Change I scream, Hallelujah! A change has come!

Change is important, if there were no variety in life and everything remained stagnate there would be no life left to live.

So whether the change is good, bad, or odd, I will take the challenge of this adjustment with arms wide open. It beats not giving me the opportunity to evolve.

This **change** feels good!

-2009-

DARKNESS
Off the back roads of
Lake Placid, FL.

Color Wheel

Red is **R**ose petals **E**ndlessly **D**ripping down
like drops of blood

Blue is **B**ruised **L**ifeless **U**tterly **E**mpty

Gray is **G**rief **R**endering **A**ssistance **Y**ielded
Purple is **P**ressure **U**rged and **R**ushed
Preventing **L**ife **E**vents

Green is **G**rowing **R**age from **E**nvy **E**veryone
Needed

Yellow is **Y**arn **E**ntertainment about a **L**ittle
Light **O**wning **W**ishes

Black is **B**lood **L**acking from **A**rtery **C**ut by
Knife

Black is the result of the mixing of all colors,
a resting place for the light.
It is the eternal night, it's the end.

-2010-

LONG ROAD AHEAD
Off the back roads of
Lake Placid, FL.

Never Been So Scared

I have never been more scared of not knowing what is ahead of me, 'til now.
I feel like everything is caving in all over me.

I can't breathe, I can't see, I can't even think clearly now.

I can't believe how far I've come, but still so scared that the end is coming near,
I can't picture myself walking down the aisle or working in a steady career.
I am so afraid that all the work I have done in school isn't going to amount to anything when I'm gone.

I can't breathe, I can't see, I can't even think clearly now.

I want to find someone to fall in love with and settle down and love forever and ever.
I want to have kids but I'm so scared, that isn't in the cards for me.

I can't breathe, I can't see, I can't even think clearly now.

I'm scared that I won't make it to 30, but at least I made it past 20.
I have never been more scared than how I am feeling right now and I just hope I can make it through this craziness somehow.

I can't breathe, I can't see, I can't even think clearly now.

-2002-

Not a Father

These eyes have cried the last tears for you.
These lungs have held the last breath for you.
These ears have heard the last promise you have made.
These hands have waved a final goodbye!

I am stronger without you here,
Maybe, now people can see me happy again.

Promises you have made,
Have turned into lies,
When will I ever hear the truth from you?
And not from a note, a card, or a phone call.
But face to face,
So I can look into your eyes!

You are too afraid,
Afraid that I will catch you on your bluff!

Here we are 22 years later, and I still don't know whether you love me
or if it is all a big hoax.

A father is suppose to give his daughter butterfly kisses… you haven't!
A father is suppose to love me unconditionally…you don't!
A father is suppose to be my protector…you are not!
A father is suppose to give me away at my wedding…you never will!

Because you are not a father,
Never were you and
Never will you ever be.

You are just a sorry excuse of a so-called man and,
Never do I wish to ever see you again!

-2002-

The Addict

She slurs, I'm alright!
It's my life, not yours!
Get out of my way!
You disgust me!
You don't know a thing!

But she is so wrong!
When I hear her spout ugly truths about me,
I feel the pain like a knife to my wrist,
I see the blood dripping down my arm.

Addictions run so deep within the both of us.

She hits the bottle,
Then her actions ruin all of her family ties!

I hit the piece of glass from that bottle,
Then all of her hurtful words run out from my screaming veins!

An addict by nature or an addict by victim

She thinks that she is far better than everyone,
While I feel like a wretched foolish loser

She is killing herself very slowly,
But I could go at any minute!

Her addiction is a curse but I can't talk mine is so much worse!

The higher she feels when that drug takes affect,
The deeper I sink into a rut of regret.

She is just a drunk is what everyone says,
But she is family and the consequences to my feelings
are more harmful than
 from a stranger.

Habits,
Problems,
Compulsions,
Impulses,
Cravings,
Needs,
Call it what you may
It all leads to...

An Addict!

She doesn't see it, yet I do so clearly.

We will both be gone before we know it,
If we don't admit to ourselves that we are addicts!

-2010-

The Step-Father by Law

He is short and ugly with long black hair.
Those who do not know him, better beware.
He is 27 years of age,
Who shouldn't have been let out of his cage!

He has evil snake eyes,
And tells vicious, vicious lies
He smiles like he's up to something
He likes to believe that he's a king.

He makes me so crazy,
Because he is so lazy
He is so inconsiderate,
And probably is illiterate.

After he said, I do,
He thought the friendship between my mom and I was through.
But little does he know,
I run the show.

And when it comes time to pull the plug,
I will surely take out this stupid want to be thug!

-1997-

TROUBLE
In my backyard in
Lake Placid, FL.

Too Much Control

You scream and yell to control this one
You push and shove to put that one in his place
You tried to control their every action
You drove them to the edge.

And there was no coming back!

You tried to control everyone around you
You scream and hit them good
You think beating common sense into them is right
But you have no clue; you are pushing them farther and farther away.

You may have done that to your own
You may have thought it was okay, because that was the way you were raised
But there comes a point where enough is enough

You may have pushed them away to the point where they will never come back!

But I have learned from them and I feel much stronger

To hurt you, like you did them,
Not with physical violence
But with the power to walk away and never turn back!

-2002-

Trapped

I feel like I'm standing in an empty black room.
One door and no windows, but

The door is...
Locked
Chained
Boarded up
And rigged close from the outside

I can't go through it,
I can't go around it,
I can't unhinge it,
It won't open!

I feel like I'm losing air,
I can't breathe!
My knees get weak,
I fall to the floor,
I cry then feel myself drowning in my own tears,

I can't breathe!
Suffocating in my fears,
Tortured by my thoughts,

Screaming in silence,
Slowly dying inside!
Alone, trapped in
My own mind!

-2008-

Untitled 2002

They tried to control me
And a part of me lets them
They say awful things
And a part of me doesn't say a word
They talk to me like I am five
And a part of me wants to cry.

But still I go back
Am I testing my limits or just plain stupid?
Am I playing into their game or have they sucked me in so for that I can't think straight?

They were pushing me to the edge
But I got stronger with each shove
They were playing with my mind
But now I play with theirs

I feel like I'm fighting a never ending war.
And just when I feel it's almost done.
They come back stronger and powerful more and more

As I fight this battle, my reinforcement comes.
As an angel watching over me, he is my knight in shining armor, and
A ray of light beams so brightly on him

To let them know,
Don't mess with a clever and powerful team.

Known as me and my Uncle Dana!

-2002-

Photograph Locations

Eerie Night- The cover photo taken in November of 2010. The location was from my front yard in Lake Placid, FL.

Trouble-This was taken in July of 2000. The location was in my backyard in Lake Placid, FL.

Stillness-This was taken in November of 2010. The location was the public boat dock area on Lake Placid in Lake Placid, FL.

Darkness- This photo was taken in November of 2010. The location was off the back roads of Lake Placid, FL.

Lonely Path-This was taken in May of 2008. The location was Cypress Gardens Adventure Park in Winter Haven, FL.

Orange Passion-This photo was taken in October of 2010. The location was off State Road 66 in Sebring, FL.

Angel Star-This was taken in October of 2010. The location was off County Road 635 in Sebring, FL.

Rushing Waters-This was taken in May of 2008. The location was Cypress Gardens Adventure Park in Winter Haven, FL.

Sticks to Break Bones-This was taken in November of 2010. The location was off the back roads of Lake Placid, FL.

Long Road Ahead- This was taken in November of 2010. The location was off the back roads of Lake Placid, FL.

Hello New Day-This photo was taken in November of 2010. The location was of Lake Jackson in Sebring, FL.

Printed in the United States
by Baker & Taylor Publisher Services